Can I

Start as beginner, End as winner

ANKIT KUMAR VERMA

Blue Rose

www.bluerosepublishers.com

First Published in September 2017

GGKEY: GK5HW82HCLN E

(ISBN- 9798730464933)/978-93-87038-72-1

ASIN-B091FF8KWB

Imprint: independently published

CAN I- Global Edition

[COPYRIGHT CONTENT]

Cover & Layout design

Danny Lincoln, Tyler Lastovich, Luana Azevedo

Unsplash

Flags in back cover denotes availability of book in country and

I respect flags of all nations

Distributed by

Blue Rose, Amazon

Preface

<Let's keep all the things aside>

First of all, thanks to select this special book

I will not say that- "this book can make your life a - change forever"

Or "this is the only book which can make your life or build your life"

Absolutely not

But in fact, if you read this book with good understanding and apply these selective strategy can help you to succeed in long run.

And talking about the second question is that applying the strategy of some more self-development books helps you to make/build your life – (better, extra or beyond) ordinary.

As regard,

With understanding the importance of your time, let start to take a great decision to make a "great" start.

I have introduces **[#shorts]** to understand the motto of each page and you can learn great lessons

INTRODUCTION

'LIFE IS A DREAM THAT COMES TRUE'

Hi!!

Champions

The book deals with different ways to express life, comparing as sorrow, beauty, song, struggle, adventure, challenge etc.

It is a book that can gives a choice to the reader to express life in its own way, and a result of experience of more than 100 of self-development, business management, and psychology books, this book will surely serve you better and *might be your best friend.*

{*Basically*}

As

Every person has a dream but...

Only few can make it happen, this book give a chance to overcome failure and moreover a way to pursue dream in life.

Notably-

When you were child you may have taken the decision of your life that what you want to become- that- what most of us does?? But...

Now, Are you that

What you think…?

….

If NO then why????

You want to achieve more in life, want fame, success, a gentleman's life and sometime a luxury life with money in your pocket a smile in your face and love in your heart then this book is surely yours,

I think YES U HAVE THE POWER TO DO GREAT IN LIFE, through your talent, skill, hard work, determination, belief etc.

Reading it as self-guide, motivation and psychology oriented book this is not an English reading book

LESSONS FOR LIFE

PART - 1

PART 2

It is the book help you to deals with the idea of mother Teresa and moreover, also the idea of being different, unique, successful, and a great personality.

— *Life*

LIFE is an opportunity, benefit from it.

LIFE is a beauty, admire it.

LIFE is a dream, realize it.

LIFE is a promise, fulfill it.

LIFE is a challenge, meet it.

LIFE is a duty, complete it.

LIFE is a game, play it.

LIFE is a sorrow, overcome it.

LIFE is a struggle, accept it.

LIFE is a song, sing it.

LIFE is a luck, make it.

LIFE IS TOO PRECIOUS, DO NOT DESTROY IT.

LIFE IS LIFE, FIGHT FOR IT …

— Mother Teresa

Dedication

To my mom Mrs. Kusum Devi and respected teachers, who were always there to help me...

WINNER'S PARTICLE MANUAL

AIM - To attain great height in life with endeavoring good values, to be extraordinary

THINGS REQUIRED - Ear to listen, mouth to read, and a brain to understand

And hence skill I will transform.

Currently

The idea of making this book short is to make you understand only the main points rather to gossips all stuffs, it is written to give you the best and makes you strong physically, mentally, emotionally and socially

Always tries to make proper plan, learn from experiences remember- success is the real Revenge

I can, thus only give you just give you 10% rather all you have to give yours 100%, which you will learn by the MASTER book

Note to my value reader

- Some pages are initially left blank in the book so that you can write your own Idea

THEORY

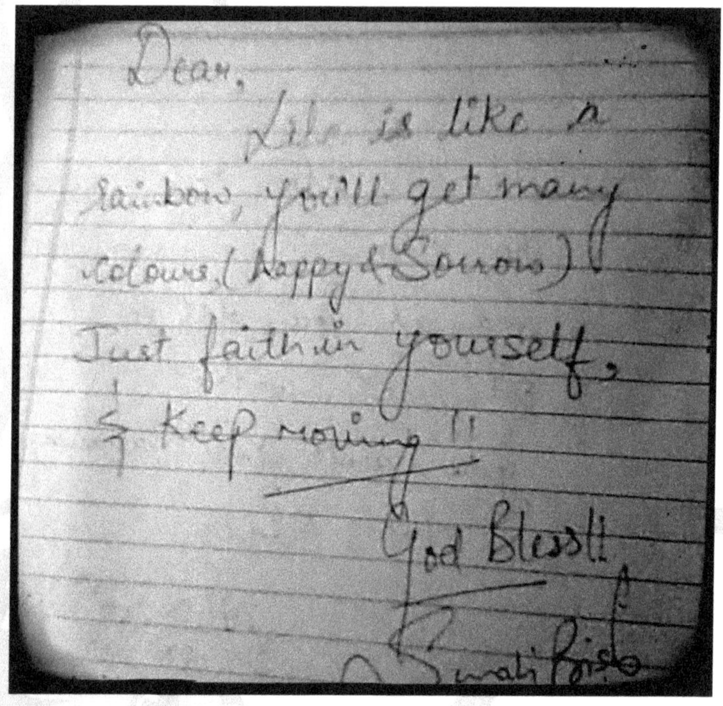

Dear,
Life is like a rainbow, you'll get many colours, (happy & Sorrow)
Just faith in yourself,
& Keep moving !!
God Bless!!

Written by an inspirational teacher

Who helped me in various phase of LIFE?

(Believe yourself and have faith in your ability)

It is not only a talent which gives you the taste success, but rather it's a hard work, determination, ability, confidence, energy, proper planning, focus, seriousness, observer, time management, willpower, uniqueness, zest and zeal is necessary to find yourself above the sky.

Because 'the one who moves alone is the who moves fast'-all the best for your rest life

I don't have the way to excel

But I believe in myself and sure

I raise high above sky…

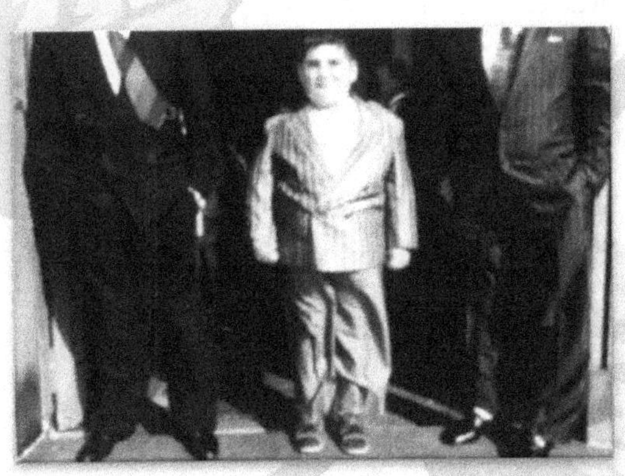

Can I be a leader!! And will make my own way

Yes!! I can.

Image source - internet

PROCEDURE

OPPORTUNITY

OP-OPPORTUNITY comes only ones but if you miss them it's not necessary that the same opportunity will come again knock the door, so be ready to fulfill the demand of opportunity and utilize it for the benefit of the society. Give your opportunity your Best way to realizes you're potential and help to overcome failure and achieve success.

Opportunity can open the door of success.

Opportunity comes to those who believe in it, who has the power to access it, we all are homo sapiens, and we have the opportunity to clear path of success, but when I compare to animals they also have the opportunity but they don't have the comfort zone they don't have the clothes to wear in cold, they don't have the fan that can help them in summer but they are accepting every challenges and make their way.

Opportunity are coming, move out from your comfort zone, and grab the opportunity.

You have got the opportunity

Don't ignore it!!!

Make it happen,

Firstly, believe in yourself and have hope to the opportunity to relies our dream that can come true

Secondly, relies your potential to make it happen to overcome your fear and to achieve success

Third, practice, practice, and practice to opt

Lastly. Research.

【Finally】

Do your present work in unexpected manner?

Perform a great hard work, surely you will find the great opportunity make use of that opportunity in such a manner that you may get better and then best.

OPPORTUNITY, OPPORTUNITY

Lies in your own hand…

Opportunity differs from person to person, it can be determined by the amount of willpower, practice, experience, and amount of self-confidence you have, to pursue your dream.

Remember – 'IN THE MIDDLE OF EVERY DIFFICULTY, LIES

An OPPORTUNITY'.

People often discuss about the opportunities they miss in life

But I will say that from today start your new day to cultivate the habit of creating and get access to your opportunity and achieve success in long run.

You merely thinks about getting high professional , white collar jobs and many more… that's the first steps, you made a mind set to your jobs, but when the time came - to do hard work on your habit and to make your dream come true- you didn't

But why?

THE SOLUTION OF THE ABOVE PROBLEM LIES IN ONLY YOUR HAND

Just believe in yourself, make adequate plan, and give it full effort = full victory, practice your good habits or weak points

Write your dream in a page and read it before you get to sleep, be positive and be serious about life.

And the most important thing is to work smartly, give it a perfect practice, get motivated and consider the aspects of victorious personalities to understand their vision.

'The best preparation for better tomorrow is to do hard work today'

So believe in yourself... [Stay calm]

Developing the attitude of psychological resilience

This simply defines the capacity to recover from difficult life event, learning and moving despite life's downturn, it enable to stay calm and focus during crisis resilience can be developed by build positive connection, through self-awareness, sleep hygiene and learning problem solving skill

Divide your mistakes, reason to fail in many small parts then put effort in every part build a full training program where you can push your limits to create mental edge, learn to coop with extreme adverse situation, pressure

[#shorts]

After losing in Wimbledon Djokovic said I will come back stronger emerge stronger from every setback

Framework

What are the 5 habits of successful people according to you?

……………………………………………………………………

……………………………………………………………………

……………………………………………………………………

……………………………………………………………………

……………………………………………………………………

……………………………………………………………………

……………………………………………………………………

PSYCHOLOGY

Scientific study of human mind and its function especially those affect behaviors.

Psychologist explores behavior and mental process including perception, cognition, attention, emotion intelligence phenomenology motivation brain function and personality.

Major subparts of psychology

Biological

Behavioral

Cognitive

Social and so on…

Psychology books helps to heals and to fight back in every situation in life.

Here one thing also matter is personality i.e. your personality should be the best to other

Psychology is the 'study of soul' we need to understand them for proper use of It., moreover its emphasis on human behavior and the importance of cognition.

Organism is any living creature. Consequently, it need to understand behavior of dogs, pigeons, and monkeys and can be legitimately included in the study of psychology.
Such organisms have indeed been subjects in psychology experiments. When animals
are used in experiments, the implicit goal is often to explore how such basic processes as learning and motivation, as studied in animals, can lit a fire on our understanding of human behavior

Scientific psychology has four explicit goals:

(1) Describe (2) explain, (3) predict, and (4) control behavior

[Learning]

Did you ever thought how doctor can perform long 20 hours of operation in emergency situation?

How an athlete can run fast after running 10 km by look at the last line

This can be how you can trick your brain to push more

Whenever you are tired your expression changes, body send signal to brain that you are really tired, at this time you can trick your brain with a BIG smile

Humor can reduce stress in dangerous and difficult situation means Optimism can increase Grit

Whenever you think its last your limit and you are out of energy just do push yourself 5 →→

5 Minute **extra** then increase by 10, 15 and more

This will create mental toughness

And build neural connection in brain, increases stamina of brain as it happens in perceived exertion

BEAUTY

'Everything has its own beauty but not everyone can see it'

Beauty is not always necessary, further it will also be right to say that- everything has a beauty but not everyone can see it. Beauty don't matter the real thing which matter is your success followed by the hard work, dedication and patience, which makes you possibly great

"Meditate. Live purely. Be quiet. Do your work with mastery. Like the moon, come out from behind the clouds! Shine."

"Is it so bad, then, to be misunderstood? Pythagoras, Socrates, and Luther, Copernicus, Galileo, Newton, and every person and wise spirit that ever took power hand by hand.

"Count your age by friends, not years. Count your life by smiles, not tears. "Don't dwell about the chance you miss

"Ever tried. Ever failed. No matter. Try Again. Fail again. Fail better."

"Here's to the crazy ones, the misfits, the rebels, the troublemakers, the round pegs in the square holes… the ones who see things differently — they're not fond of rules… You can quote them, disagree with them, glorify or verify them, but the only thing you can't do is ignore them because they change things… they push the human race forward, and while some may see them as the crazy ones, we see genius, because the ones who are crazy enough to think that they can change the world, are the ones who do."

— Steve Jobs

Beauty can be 100%, but it matters both external and internal beauty. External beauty counts only 10%. Give your 90% to internal beauty and rest 10% will be the always the best in you. THE POWER LIES IN YOUR HAND TO MAKE YOUR DREAM COME TRUE.

'''

Self-doubt can create problem in your life, follow a perfect routine, and focus at the solution rather than problem

Exercise on your weakness to make your dream come true and relies your potential.

Positive affirmation can be helpful in this part

Bob Proctor says *I am so happy and grateful now that…*

I continuously stretch myself

To create a life that is full of Success and Satisfaction {Self-esteem statement}

2. I believe in myself, have confidence to acquire success, have power to raise above limits to excel in life and that is possible because I am one in a million, and different or unique

Make your own affirmation from below point while writing

1. Feel the result in present
2. Honest demand
3. Never use negative word in affirmation
4. Confirm the result
5. Most important is consistency

Framework

Why hard work is difficult, playing tough game is addictive in nature

Working on difficult task creates mental fatigue instead playing tough game in interesting

....

....

....

....

....

....

Write your own thoughts

DREAM

TO BE THE BEST IN LIFE

I have a dream, what dream do you have?? Share it by your relative or friends make your dream come true in life, accept challenge in life

Because life gives you result as a plant, what you sow in the soil of the era LIFE

Everybody has a dream in life but not everybody can pursue them, you have got the opportunity to make your dream come true, you have the talent to make it true so from today work hard to make your dream come true…

What is the purpose in your life? Relies it

Everybody has a dream, you must the one have a "living dream" which can transform into reality

Have a dream which can be come true so work hard on it now, ask some question to yourself

What is the purpose in your life?

What is your goal in life? And why you want to go for it.

-What are the things that can help in making your life successful?

-What are your plans in life, Goals to achieve?

Once you answer these question

Raise your hand with a smile and say loudly yes- I can

I will be a winner

{Read it, as yours}

My life gave me another opportunity to raise, fly in life **can I** be a leader ... **Can I** be successful as other people are??

Can I make my dream true can I make my promise fulfill can I be a winner.

YES!!! I CAN BE the WINNER IN MY LIFE

I WILL SURELY BECOME SUCCESSFUL IN MY LIFE

I WILL BE UNIQUE I WILL BE A WINNER

DREAM BIG IN LIFE

MAKE YOUR OWN WAY TO BE PERFECT IN YOUR OWN LIFE

Do something great, so that people can remember you even you are not there -considering right way

Don't go where the path lead, make your own path and leave a trail there are enormous examples in the world, they never died, they are alive in every way. Why?

Because they are able to see their life and world in different way which makes them unique, great. Then why you can't do it, as you are also a human

Problem are the part of life problem are compulsory in life. How you make it and fight from it makes you a winner

Ones you excel, soar high and high in life, there will no problem

[Instead]

But there will be a challenges which you have to overcome to make your life more meaningful

"Defeat the defeat before it defeat you"

[#shorts]

THE Rule is same either you are leader of 10 people or leader of 10,000 people

PROMISE

Promise is someone's believe, may depends but never break promises of anyone either it can be, Friend relative or your parent and especially to yourself-believe in yourself, have faith in your ability while some used says 'Promise is made to be broken' then, it doesn't stand for promise and it don't define promise-

You have a promise to keep, so make your promise true, and help them to make those wonderful event

Trust is built on the series of experiences shared with other, when promises are misled, the bond of trust are breached

JUST BELIEVE IN YOURSELF AND KEEP MOVING IN LIFE

Never break promise of other because promise is the trust that is given to a person on behalf…

So never, never break promise it can destroy, damage your relations or reputation

Promise are the important parts of one's life

TAKE CARE OF YOUR promise to do something greater in life because you promise is necessary in life to aspect, Bigger than anything.

Life is promise, fulfill it…

For teacher- a promise to teach great habits to young minds not only young minds but also everyone's as equal.

For lawyer is a promise to do justice to and for the people and helps them to overcome.

For police promise is to make people, city free from crimes.

And helps them to get their right and treat them equal and get the theft behind the bar. Think about your promise.

Never, never, never break promise of other because when somebody believes you he or she has a faith in you so, never make them upset and break trust of other.

Make your life as such people get inspire from you, takes you as to follow their dream when get inspire from you.

'We all are dreaming of success, but the winner will woke up work hard to achieve it'

So, BE A WINNER, NEVER BREAK PROMISE IN LIFE

Everybody has someone important in life to makes someone happy I mean when they look at you, a true positive smile comes out either it be a parents or anyone important in your life care their promise

There were many dogs barking at your path of success and people may say you many thing but before trying anything ask yourself three question

1. What I'm doing is it a right thing??

2. Can it help to reach my goal?

3. What will be its result?

Lastly thinks about your parents

'The past is prove that nobody is perfect, and future is the prove that everyone is a change'

Thinking is most powerful always think positive. You always have a hidden power within you. Never compare yourself with other, you are the best.

CHALLENGES

Challenges are the part of life, essential in our life they are the test paper as in your life.

Life is a challenge, accept it…

'Challenges are what make the life interesting, and overcoming them is what makes LIFE meaningful'

Take every challenge as a chance to make you proof that you are the POWER

Every person has a challenge in life few to get food, to get money, to be on the top, to get fame to achieve and to be a winner

{Compare}

Have you saw an ocean tides, they crushes the stones in their path same way break the difficult situation, access the power to cultivate success

As every person has to travel the road of challenge few take them more importantly!!

While some people take it as a joke and their life tends to be a joke

Every winner has to take challenge and defeat the defeat before it defeat you.

Make a great, powerful target in life and accepts responsibilities and defeat all the challenges in life, it's your life make it large

GET YOUR CHALLENGES DEFEATED BY YOU

"Challenge yourself with something you know you could never do and what you will find that you will overcome come anything"

It's a great method to find you above your limits {read it once more}

Challenges are the art of life accept it. Which make success available or enjoyable

Parents, friends, you teachers has a belief in you and are waiting enough someone who can make their life better they trust you, they have a hope that yes!! This is my child he or she will become a successful person of tomorrow's generations, so never break their trust and accept responsibility and achieve great heights in life. Always learn from ideas, the story of successful people and strugglers moreover failures.

<u>No matter how you feel, get up; dress up, and</u>

<u>Never give up</u>

[#shorts]

Leader should have multiple source to gather information they should not depend on one source permanently

DUTY

DUTY has its responsibility to obey or to enrich the value of life to excel great in life. Everybody has certain kind of duty but are you following them???

{If you salute your duty you don't need to salute anyone but if you pollute your duty you need to salute everyone.}

Follow your duty in better way ...

If you don't have duty in life, how can you achieve in your life,

[Compare]

Have you ever notice an ant how an ant follows the duty to perform better and better in everyday in her life. An ant knows his duty well -as a creature she believe in hard work she carry food for their family and keep trying

When she get slipped from the wall - again tries, and further.

[Experiment]

When an ant is moving on the surface keep a small wooden block in front of them they will either try to cross it by climbing on it or by taking another path

Learn from them…

<u>Note- don't harm them</u>

Act correctly when the problem comes, we have to move across to make a new path for living in a better way have you act as an ant above, think upon it once …

Everybody has his own duty because but…some of them don't accept it or don't perform it.

You might think duty is boring every day same work and you might think why to be more vigilant? Make your duty to help other

These are some typical type of problem you may face but you may don't the right solution but believe I can give you give you some useful tips that you may don't know

.firstly make a new beginning of every magnificent kind of things you are doing be more smart like working on common sense it may take some days to build, you can use a candle to focus it, in a silence zone for 2 to 3 min… after 30 to 40 days, you will yourself relies some great powers, concentration, if you carry this, you will be more focused. Same in a slot make new every day and take interest in what are you are doing.

Secondly, perform your duty well do great even in

Small things perform a small thing but in a great way because,

A WHOLE JOURNEY BEGINS WITH A SINGLE STEP "

LASTLY, the most common thing that people don't get success is that they don't try at all. Make your own success story don't copy other. Never give up

Most importantly the best source to attempt success and motivate yourself is belief system, if you have believe that yes!! You can achieve success, no one can stop you

GAME

LIFE IS A GAME PLAY FOR IT.

Life doesn't count that how much you live it rather count, how many times it takes your breath always by the critical situation. It's your life make it as such a way that everybody compare yourself with you and wants to be like you.

The more you will be active the more you will be strengthen, you be energetic.

You are a player and you must is a play for your life.

Remember that the pain you feel today is the strength you feel tomorrow your LIFE is very important don't waste, well enjoy every moment and achieve high goals in LIFE.

IT'S NOT ABOUT WINNING OR LOSSING IT'S ALL ABOUT PLAYING THE GAME AND ENJOING EVERY PHASE OF LIFE

But remember; those who knows how to win are more numerous, than those who make proper use of their victory,

Play like a winner excel like a winner and be a winner of our life

HERE are the few thing a helps you to get ahead of all the stuffs-

Make decision in life but in systematic manner by listening to the majority and sometime core of the heart.

Believe in yourself, listen you inner voice, go for your dream what you thought in past but in right way

People may say you idiot, foolish, mental they may discard you from your path but remember you are still the master of your heart and leader of your soul

Have faith in your ability, just believe in yourself work hard silently, the world will be at your feet.

Never forget humanity in your life accept failure and try for a next success.

Go for your DREAM and make your own success story.

#shorts

Daily commitment is most vital part in a day, if you have commitment and consistency in your work then the time will work for you

George RR martin teaches you the power of consistency that how to deal with failure and be consistent in every situation, failure should not affect your consistency

~~initially book was flop, martin continues to write in every end day and finally drafted the best book game of thrones, martin has a computer which cannot even send mail, the only thing martin computer can do is WRITE - and that makes him Distraction free, that makes him to focus on one things

So, **what is your minimum to succeed?**

………………………………………………………

………………………………………………………

………………………………………………………

………………………………………………………

………………………………………………………

………………………………………………………

………………………………………………………

I tried to keep it very simple, somebody lives in the present I don't think too much about the past or future that I have kept saying

I have learning from the past and of course you need to have goals for future but…

I know the most important thing is the present whatever I do in the present creates an impact in future because we all go through almost the same thing

But at the end of the day to reach your mark, you have to struggle in life and it's all circumstances, small decision that you've to make that actually have a big impact in life

-MS DHONI

STRUGGLE

Life is all about challenges. How you respond to it makes your life meaningful, makes it large (life) struggle is necessary but in right direction.

-pulling, pushing applying force on wall, working hard without any motto don't counts.

What are the things you will be remember for make it happen, all you have a page in history can help to find your goal.

Make that thing happen in history believe me everyone can be a leader but there is an issue that if everyone becomes a leader then who will be clapping audiences, you should believe in yourself, work hard and smart both, acquire continuous knowledge and have patience to overcome mountain and be a leader

Struggle is the part of life you just have to stand like a soldier, struggle add taste and flavor to your victory.

Make your own success story have power to excel, fulfill your dream and attain greatest height so that everyone your parents, friends, relative, teacher can proud on you and say that my… is a YOU MOST SUCCESSFUL PERSON EVER.

You need a live your dream to succeed and you have to follow that path. A struggle is the most important part of life remember , all successful people struggle in early way of success, they clear most of the struggle in their way, believe me the more you struggle, the more better way you find to solve the problem, the more successful you will be.

The winner don't do different things, they do it

They do it exceptionally...

"Challenges are what makes your life, interesting and overcoming them is what make it meaningful"

Everyone in the universe can get succeed on after travelling the path of struggle you can take any example {Respected} -MARRY KOM, LINCON, EINSTEIN, WASHINGTON, BOB MARLEY, ABDUL KALAM, ANURIMA SINHA, MOTHER TERESA etc.

Challenges are the part of your life, you have to crush them alone

The power lies in your hand you have to travel that road of struggle if you want to taste the real flavor of success, no one can else travel, and you have the power to be the difference, accept challenges be the power to serve millions

Use whatever you have- what things you have doesn't matters it only matter is that

How?

You attempt struggle to make the history have believe in yourself so first believe yourselves have faith in your ability.

DON'T BE THE CROWD BE THE LEADER TO SERVE THE CROWD, make your own way the else will follow because the lion refuse to walk with the sheep's make own way and stand alone?

(Have you ever notice cats that when they get the tastes of milk… they become passionate about. So they will visit again, if you catch them then also they get to visit again. Be passionate. Likewise when once you get the taste of success you will hit another aim definitely again and again, BE PASSIONATE ENOUGH)

{Observed}

Your success rate can be determine by the 5 person you surround with i.e. It must be a good company, a good friends, we generally make friends similar to us rather make friend those have god value, discipline in them that really affects your life otherwise change your habit.

Bad company and friendship can destroy your life, they have low esteemed and values and moral are substandard and by this value they cannot do well in life they will put you down, this can affect ones life and you will become substandard

Here are some behavioral aspect of substandard person

-worst hygiene

-envious and complain type

-if he is not open to very close persons like best friend

-Always thinks below the belt, bad intentions

-hurting innocent people

You should immediately get rid of such persons if they have 3 or more of these abominable qualities

Build your good personality try to be the man of values Noble people will attracted by benevolent nature and positivity.

#shorts

Quality is trumps Quantity

SONG

Life is like a song, sing for it

When you're happy, try to make other also, because it is the thing which makes you more than how happy you are.

From happiness to song

Song plays an important part in your life as it determine your mood when you are happy don't make any promise and when you are sad or angry don't make any decision

You can be the millions dreams just be the best respects your elder respect, your parents because your parents makes you a winner keeping their life in trouble reads books take good habit ignore the bad habits revising the above advice, you may heard daily at the time, when you were young

We all are born to do something great life just do it as you are also a winner be different, be unique.

Make your dream, set your goal set your target if you have MONOMONICAL MADNESS then nobody on the earth can stop you,

Yes!! If you are mad about your passion, your dream, no one can stop you to reach them

[You may]

These all things I have said you in the book just depend on you either you want to take it or not ignore it see I can only say you motivate you show you the right path it depend on you either you ignore it or absorb it

Don't just read absorb it to get instant success

ROSE is famous for grace, advocate is famous for his case

Horse is famous for his race, and you are famous for your smile so,

Keep smiling

Stay ahead, win every game

ONCE

A man asked Lord Buddha "**I WANT HAPPINESS**"

Buddha replied- first remove **I** -that's ego

Then, remove **WANT** that's desire. See now you are left with "**HAPPINESS**"

Make a list your habits forming schedule and a list that can serve you greatly that has itself a great advantages in it.

An exemplary edition is created below

- ✓ Work on physical exercise and yoga.
- ✓ Learn different languages.
- ✓ To practice writing with different hand.
- ✓ To read good books
- ✓ To work on weakness
- ✓ To work on my goals.

Note –

- You have to make this list a day before, in case if the habits a changing on daily basis *for example* –To read books.
- Maintain the sequences as priority

LUCK

There is nothing like luck on how much you prepare makes your luck.

'The better you prepare the luckier you get'

But some time it can prove in in a very small ratio

If in a situation you thought that you may clear an exam only because of your luck and on the other hand your friend is give his 1000% to it and he is probably thinks that he will definitely be the first and topped the exam as a sure sort vision and hard word which can lead to strong foundation.

The best to prepare is to have faith in yourself, hard work, determination, patience and clarity

(To be extra from ordinary–reaches to find extraordinary)

Try to present yourself as such that peoples cannot see your weak points rather they see as strong as their role model in life just

Have faith in your ability. Life is not about winning and get ahead, just stand in front of mirror and say , one day I will be the most successful, lovely, happier, wealthier person in the world, I am the best I will be a good leader

The whole world will be beneath you just believe in two things in life just believe in two things i.e.

HARD WORK + ENERGY =SUCCESS

(In right direction and under right coach)

It is the only first level definition of success.

"There are only 24hr in each day how we use makes the difference"

Get away from the person says negative thing about society or you need get away from that person because he who run fast, who walks alone.

Remember, if you call out and nobody comes WALK alone

(Revised)

'Get away from the person says negative thing about society or you need get away from that person' but if in the case, you are the target is you and an individual is saying to you then make point for it and try to cure it as they can search your weak point more clearly

Note-it must be your weakness- that can be cured but away from social, violence

There is nothing like luck only is that your preparation of hard work and determining makes you powerful.

PART -2

MOST BENEFICIAL.

SUMMARY

Note -Nothing is common about words in this summary compared to above things it is a quite important part of this book

- Success, the path of life which deals with the way to work hard, talent, patience ,struggle, sacrifice, believe in your ability to attract success its depend on person's potential and vary from person to person . Make mistakes learn from them.
- "Wake up work hard and make your dream come true in reality"
- Practice the power in perfect way, Work hard have faith, start your success journey from today it is the- right, perfect, and the best Time.
- Don't blame on time do it today in a right now you don't have resource make own resource you have resourcefulness in hidden you

Show the world that YOU CAN!!

Be the history Maker.............................!!!

Success is a word that may vary from person to person the right decision at right time makes you a winner, moreover, find out the possible outputs of you hard work, remember you can do anything in right way to achieve success in LIFE.

Never wait for the opportunity, make your dream come true remember the days when you were young your parents, teacher has a belief in you that YOU CAN achieve why? Are you making their dream come true by achieving yours you. Resource don't matter you have it or not make your own path to achieve Grand success what I can do is to show you the right path you own have to travel it yours remember never, never GIVE UP.

When you were young that means a child you, might, thought to become a doctor, engineer scientist, pilot etc... but what you are today, ponder on it.

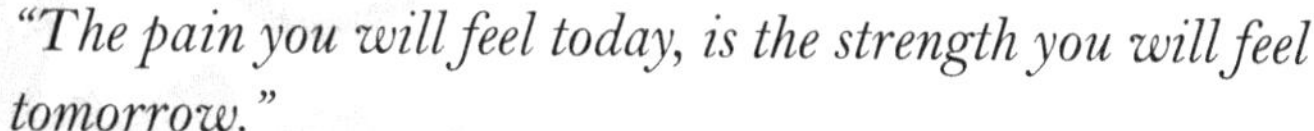

"The pain you will feel today, is the strength you will feel tomorrow."

Parents are like the Gardner and as regard you are a flower of the garden, think about their hard work patience and dedicated effort toward the little flower to make them a perfect one but felt very sad when their dreams are broken all their effort lose in one go.

Never break promise of your parents they are the most important person in your life remember, the day when your mom was happy just close your eyes and try to remember the happy face of your mother, think if they come to know that all their effort of earlier days was the waste of time on you.

Your parents also have a problem but they doesn't tell you, do you know

Why??

Because they don't want you to be upset or worry about the problem......\

You still have a chance make a smile on your parents face. It's never too late if the situation is worst

If you have any problem their remembrance of your parents can give you unmatched power…….

Attempt success in such a way that you opponent, your enemy even a success should clap and praise you.

CHILD OF A POOR FAMILY WILL BE THE ONE TO ASK FOR A JOB BUT THE ONE WHO GIVES JOBS TO THE MILLIONS.

What a son/Daughter things about his or her parents at different ages (mostly)…

4 years- My parents is great.

6 years-My parents knows everything.

10 years- My parents is short tempered

12 years- My parents was very nice when I was young

15 years- My parents is not at the current line

17 years- My parents don't understand me

How can I walk with my parents, my friends are so smart nice dressed, active, but my parents…it very shame full

18 years- My parents ohh!! How can I manage?

21 years- My parents is objecting everything

25 years- My parents No, way I can't manage him anyway

<u>After marriage</u>

30 years- My god it is very difficult to manage my son

35 years- I am puzzled that how my dad manage me? How he brought me up.

45 years- My parents face so many problem to bring me up

I am not able to manage single son

55 years- My parents was so far sighted and planned he is the best, unique DAD.

57 years- My parents is great…

Thus, it took 56 year to complete the cycle and reached to the first stage so, realize the true value of your parents before it become, too late…

Source- internet

Write your thoughts here

HABIT

Habits are the most important point in our life which tells about your personality your communication skill your habits are what that can make you successful a good leader in your life, so you first need to check your habit i.e. on daily basis. If you want to make a new habit of something, then practice it for 30 days for the early morning hour it will come in your habit

(Revised)

If you want to make a new habit of something, then practice it for 30 days for the early morning hour, or an hour, time when your minds are quite active

Habit of getting late - don't be, tried to make your timetable accordingly so that there much time one minute late is better to have 1 hour early, this negative habit make a wrong staring personality

Habit of making time table only few have these habit I want you all should have time table in different way like- what I need to do tomorrow, what are the most important, important and least important work to do today. Make your time table accordingly because it is difficult to change bad habit.

HOW

To be a good **communicator**, one needs to:

a) Express own ideas clearly
b) Develop good relationships
c) Giving constructive feedback
d) Respect attitudes and opinions of others
e) Be tolerant to different customs and cultures
f) Be a good listener.
g) One should have a good questioning skill

Subjects areas

— Philosophy, psychology
— Auxiliary science of history
— World history
— History of a particular country
— Geography, Anthropology
— Political science
— Law
— Communication
— Managements
— Business/trading
— Music
— Fine arts
— Language and literature
— Science
— Agriculture
— Technology/ML
— Biology

Giving an important part i.e. quotes which will encourage you

Given by some of the famous personalities.

Quotes are taken from various sources of internet to help and to motivate Reader

THOUGHTS

Quotes are the most important parts of our life it teaches us, builds us and creates a strong foundation to stand at the top

1. "What lies behind us what lies before us are the tiny matter compared to what lies within us"

It's always not the matter of showoff is sometime get crucial to express our inner beauty

2. Challenges yourself with something you know you could never do, and what you find is that you can overcome anything's.

Challenges are important to test your preparation stand strong everybody face it.

3. it's never too late to be what you might have been

Start from where you are what you have you have enough resource to grow up as a winner.

All your dream can come true if you have courage to pursue them

Dream everything have courage to accept difficulties and stand strong to travel in right path of your dream.

Those who know how to win are more numerous than those who make proper use of victory.

A person should have –

Ability, attitude, practice, approach, attention, body language, behavior, confidence, clarity of thoughts, discipline, dedication, determination, experience, etiquette, energy, ethics, focus, guidance, health, hard work, helpful, judgmental, knowledge, learning, optimistic, judiciousness, leadership, patience, punctuality,

Rational thinking, uniqueness, willpower, zest zeal…

Stay claim,

Plan your game to win

You've plan to make and win

An a action to take and leap

It won't be the same,

When you get the fame,

For winning every GAME.

Life and time are the best two teacher life teaches us the use of time and Time teaches us the value of life.

Never play with time use your time well. Take right decision in right time.

Winning horse doesn't know why he runs in a race it runs because of beat and pain life is a race and god is your rider so when you are in pain think god wants you to win in life.

Remember the pain you feel today is the strength you feel tomorrow

The first step in success is wisdom of silence, second is listening, third is memory the fourth is practice, and fifth is to teaching others.

History is the cyclic poem written upon the memories of time.

Be the history maker

Read it ones it is very important it is actually the mixture of all thoughts don't get confuse after every

THE NEW WAY

(…) there is another sentence with different meaning .try to understand each line correctly and surely

Excellent is never an accident, result of high intention, it is always the sincere effort and intelligent execution... The better you prepare the luckier you get…there is very little difference between people. And that make a big difference the little difference is attitude and big difference is it is either positive or negative…know your strength exercise them…do not go where the path lead but make you own path and leave a trail, because the winner stand-alone…hope for the best be prepare for the worst…judge not those who fail and try but judge those who fails and try I will not win immediately but definitely…believe in your ability have faith in yourself…

Challenge yourself to something you know you could never do and what you will find that you will overcome anything…life is 10 % what happen to you and 90% how you react with it… if you cannot do great things do small thons in great way…a journey of thousand miles begins beneath one foot…the best preparation is to do hard work today… one machine can do the work of 1000 ordinary men but no machine can do a work of 1 extra ordinary man…

LIVE the life you want to live

Be the person you want to be to be remembered

Make decision make mistake

IF you fall, at least you tried…

Lastly, write your dream it is one of the most important thing write your dream in a copy and read it once in a day

Motivate yourself by saying that yes!! I CAN, I WILL, I DO- ACHIEVE SUCCESS NOT IMMEDIATELY BUT DEFINITELY and start practicing today to achieve you goal because todays hard work can give you the taste of success in future and have a full energy and clarity in mind to achieve desire goal. Get out of your comfort zone to achieve success

Don't worry about failure it is important in life because-

"Those only fails who tries, they don't fail who don't try"

Never tell a person a person that something is not possible. God may have weighting for centuries for somebody ignorant enough to impossible to do that things

- All written by some of the great personalities

STUDY SKILLS

SKILLS change that our life as winds.

Studying is the process that is used to decide what to learn and what to remember and recall

— James F Shepherd

The only time an exam should be a trial is when you aren't prepare for it. And the best sign you are prepare in exam hall is to have calm and unnecessary talk should be avoided. Just close your eyes and recall all your mistake, you have done previously and make sure that you should not repeat it again. Believe in yourself stay calm,

Sharp at study

Creating environment – avoid disturbance create a good study zone, a comfort straight back chair and appropriate desk. Never study at bed

Timetable – make plan accordingly, make the plan of the day at the day before make 3 column of most important, important and not important.

Survey maps - make overall picture of your book you are going to study before you start studying. Alike we made a road map before travelling.

Read – when you read actively and make small notes that can be useful in exam time, be alert to bold and italicized prints. Don't read many books of same subject (school) it may confuse you or read one book but you should read it full. Because every book as a best part in it which you may miss.

{Revised}

But when you are fully done with one book then only move to another.

Reading is a good habit read plenty of books - self-development, personality development, psychology, physics and moreover which you like

Ask-Question- Ask yourself question as you read or study and answering them can make you feel confident.

Review - Give a survey of what you have cover ant use summary to get it, recover the best time to review when just you finished studying

Take-Breaks – take creative breaks to give rest to your mind take a deep breath near a way of nature, or listen a song…

Break might be of 5-6 minutes only after every 45 minute counts.

Before exam don't panic as all concept must be cleared revise formula solve sample, mock paper in mathematics don't try to solve question especially in math's before a day of examination rather revise only problem question

Make all necessary things get ready one day before the exam.

Sleep at leat7-8 hour a day to make mind to work actively.

Physical exercise, which makes us also mentally strong

Take proper diet, eat healthy balance diet. Eating well help you to focus and do your best

Avoid going to exam with empty stomach.

Spicy food red meat soft drinks fried food should be avoided.

Include food rich in iron, zinc, iodine like fruits and vegetable, which help to build your concentration and reduce stresses.

Below are the very important tools which you can use to get definite success

LIFE TOOLS

Write your dreams – it is one the best habit, write your dreams and read it daily it can help you to reach clarity. It can be more than one destination to reach

Followed by -

I want to get good grades in this exam

I want to get the treasury of money wealth

I want to be a successful author

I want to become ---- in life

I want to get admission in -------- college

I want to have a good sports bike …

And sincerely I will put all my effort and stand as a WINNER.

Do meditations – it help to purify your mind and give you a good concentration, meditation has a long lasting effect. In our body and give us enormous power. It can be done in peace at the open space, surrounded by fresh air which makes your full day lovely.

Meditation has many benefits like –

Reduce stress and anxiety.

Improve concentration and self-awareness.

Encourage a healthy life style.

Increase happiness.

It slow aging

Reduce alcohol and substance abuse.

Gives you psychological emotional intelligence.

Reduce risk of heart disease.

Reduce blood pressure.

Make you live longer

Power of 15- take fifteen minute from your daily busy schedule and try some of the skills like-

Painting

Dancing

Exercise

Reading self-development book

Thinking.

English learning etc…

15 minute each day can be a huge amount i.e.

15*30 = 450 minutes

15*365 =5475 minute

That can give good direction on your Aim

Braine principle

Use brain to think – when you have any problem in life I will give you the best method to resolve it. It's all but how your mind things the best answer should be chosen to make you a satisfied this method is useful in any case where you need best answer by the core your heart is that-

When you get to sleep in bed and just close your eyes keep you mind peaceful and thinks only about the matter you need and you will find the best answer

Mind as alarm – you can use your mind an alarm i.e.

You just have to stay calm don't take stress on that day and at night calmly, go for sleep and say 5-6 time in your heart that I need to awake early; by tomorrow morning see the result

If you want to manage your time- the important strategy to manage your time is to a day before make list of your all important thing i.e. make plan of your next day on a night before...

If you have any bad habits like smoking consumption of alcohol etc. and you want to get rid then the best way is to write all your bad activities in page and stick it on the door, table, fridge where you daily visit and your mind can became aware of its harmful effects---

For example- consumption of alcohol

Write as it – I am a great personality that need to take care of myself because surely tomorrow I'll change the country and if I will consume it toxic, dangerous thing then what will happen to my rest of the people

OR write its effects

Organize workshop – make your own program make target like a 10 day to achieve creativity or 20 day workshop in which you will speed up my personalities

Or say communication or up to this day I will learn a new language.

Then a positive statement to you- say it four to five time a day like

I'M THE WINNER I SHALL NOT FEAR OF FAILUREs in life BECAUSE I can make my own way and I am an achiever

YOU CAN MAKE YOUR OWN SELF STATEMENT

BUSINESS SKILLS

Companies in market–

Google Alibaba Audi

Adidas Flipkart

Walmart Microsoft Heinz

General motors Reliance Samsung

Apple

Toshiba Toyota

Bmw Infosys Videocon

Amazon Facebook Ford

And many more...

Are some of the biggest brands?

Sharp you skill at which you are the best

Don't waste your time about your weak skill rather give them little time.

We will overview some of the top company---

Adobe

American multinational computer Software Company

Headquarter-

San jose, California

CEO

Shantanu Narayan

Audi

German automobile company

Founder- Augus Horch in 1910

Four rings show union of four company

First left hand drive car

CEO- Rupert stadler

Also produce race cars

Google

Birthday- unknown

CEO- Sundar Pichai

American multinational company

Products- YouTube, chrome, maps etc.

Specialized in internet related company

Toshiba

Company of japan

Founded on **1875**

204000 employees

Global network off 740+ company

Products- storage printing etc.

Headquarter- Tokyo

Ceo- Satoshi Tsunakawa

Patanjali

Patanjali Ayurveda limited is an Indian FMCG company

Headquarter- Haridwar

Ceo- Acharya Balkrishna

IBM

- International business machine
- **Head quarter-** Armonk, new York
- Over 380,300 employees
- **Invention of IBM-**
  Automated teller machine
  Floppy disk
  SQL language
  Magnetic strip card
  And many more

Source- internet

"If you talk to a man in a language he understands, that goes to his head. If you talk to him in his language that goes to his heart"

Note-Foremost you need to follow a business book to seek detail knowledge.

Important--

Each point has a deep meaning try to find them

Pro-Tips

1. Keep yourself aware and moreover updated, stay motivated, learn new skills, and exercise on your weakness.

2. Environment matters in business but the good thing is that it can change *under strong influence.*

3. Make yourself socially active, be ready for challenges exercise well on your current- research or plan to achieve -to fight in every situation.

4. Anything can be made

-Stable

-Better

-Cheap, means not very costly

Respond according to your market and products.

5. Work to inherit long lasting memory that can help you to a build great relationship.

Can you recall the name of the person you met last night, last week or last month?

If No!!

Then, this can affect your business relations.

How?

The individual can have a negative impression on you

Illustrated below-

If you call with his name (for friends and younger's)

Hi!! ***Alex*** *how are you,*

-That can have a positive impression on him that shows you cares about him.

6. Gather parties and various events or seminars with your coworkers or team members

Etiquettes for business

1. Arrive on time
2. Dress appropriately
3. Work on your body language
4. Don't interrupt in between
5. Work on communication skills
6. Quick approach to ideas and emotions

7. Change behavior, pattern according to the changing market
8. Be highly curious. to accept knowledge
9. Remember people pay for to—

   -Avoid pain

   -Solve problem

   -happiness

'Winners don't do different things they do it differently'

10. Every state has its own economic zone, sell your product to that central zone from where the supply begins, then it will be distributed all over the state…
11. Chose distributes wisely.
12. In early startup, check accessibility and all other parameter of your product by selling it in small marked and observe the response.
13. Use modern and latest technology
14. As delivery is the most integral part of many business. So the next time when your transportation is in worst condition, or fails apply these-
15. Late delivery of your product is the most common examples people shares; so why didn't you hire more drivers for long ways.
    Let us understand with an example-
    If company- A has driver that can travel max by 5 km then he need rest of two hours and some meals, it can be helpful in short distance. But it long distance - a company can hire a driver after every 5 km, who can make the chain possible by another 5 km and then by other that can save it's much time.

16. When a company went for a business meeting with large gathers then

One single room can be share by the two members of same company where it has a following benefits –

- Save the total expenditures
- More discussion of ideas.
- Eliminated the feeling of loneliness
- Helpful of both the employees and a company.

17. Smell of your product can affect its sale
really
Why not…

Smell that can feel the presence of their past, that has a smell related to their past, that can touch the core of their heart. (Depending upon your product)

Many famous business startups fails at initial times

But they start with new powers…

Failure are the pillars of success

Furthers are some step you need to take to ensure that the business is legally protected -

Prevention is better than cure

- Appointing legal adviser
- Getting a trade mark
- Partnership agreement-the memorandum of associating and article of association containing name, address of business, shareholders
- Legal document containing objective, terms and condition or responsibilities of the person involve.
- Important documents like *founder's agreement, service contacts, and private product contact* -etc.
- Get necessary license and permits
- Get a tax identification number –it simply tracks your company transactions
- Non-disclosure clause –that contain all companies information details and plans that should remain confidential.
- Discuss all the policies and procedure with your company and employee and ensure that they sign a document indicating you've had discussed all the related terms and conditions moreover receive a copy of your company hand book containing policies and procedure

Note to my valued reader- This previous list covers the basic essential and is not exhaustive. It does not cover every type of legal protection you may need. You can further contact legal adviser for more details, the information provided is not legal advice, doesn't constitute a lawyer referral service moreover some thoughts and quotes are taken from internet to help the reader to get motivated. This is psychology book which help reader to get inspiration, not an English grammar book

Motivational stories

I've tried to share with you with the most successful people which you probably don't know …

ARNOLD SCHWARZENEGGER

Arnold accomplished what he desire what he did is different from other success story he gained fame as a body builder using a launching point become a huge Hollywood star later the government of California. From body builder to blockbuster action star to comedy king to politician motive us as a young Austrian boy follows his every dream

-Born in July 30

- From the young age want to become a bodybuilder his ambition was to become the greatest bodybuilder.

-studied marketing at the university of Munich.

-His success continued as he picked up the title of

'Mr. Olympia' seven times and Mr. Universe five times.

-Attempt at a movie career were in low budget movie such as 'Hercules in New York' in 1969.

-'stay hungry' big break comedy movie to won golden globe for best action debut in motion picture

And act successfully in various movie like terminator, total recall and kindergarten.

-more recently Arnold ran in the California election or government and won, becoming the 38th governor in 2003.

ARUNIMA SINHA

As a national volleyball player she has a possession of an indomitable spirit.

-when few robbers pushed her out of the moving train in 2011, resulting a serious injury, not only one train but forty nine train moved over her left leg and she keep screaming in pain, she decided to fight back by the situations

-peoples were looking at her but nobody came forward

Then she decided to prove herself that she can be a winner to make her dream came true and she made a decision, that she would climb Mount Everest,

-for next two years she trained continuously in mountain, worked very hard there were no Sunday, every day was a working day, and day by day she is becoming better and better

- Mistake, problem, struggle, challenges, she defeated them all

But despite odd, she create a history first amputee to successfully conquer Mount Everest with artificial leg

AB DE VILLIERS

Story of a boy who was excellent at three sports

Fans of AB de Villiers look forward to hear the story

-the boy who was excelled at tennis, rugby and cricket,

- The youngest who make recodes ad make his international debut at the age of 20 and was selected in every single test played by South Africa

LEONARDO DA VINCE

Da Vince was a painter, designer, scientist of his time .Vince has a wide range of knowledge of many subjects

Da Vince is probably famous for his painting which everyone has heard - Mona Lisa's painting

Leonardo da Vince was born in April 5, 1452

Da Vince was an architect, sculptor, musician, inventor, anatomist, geologist, botanist and a writer.

Da Vince has been the first person to record the discovery of a rare fossil called paleodictyon

Da Vince has made major development in robotics, flight safety, helicopter, telescope, lenses scuba diving, anatomy, dentistry and many more…

MOTHER TERESA

She lived a life of sacrifice, love and kindness. She worked for the uplifting of society. Mother Teresa branched out from the main church and started her own diocesan congregation which subsequently became Missionaries of Charities

Mother strongly believed that love is the most powerful weapon. Her aim was to uplift "the hungry, the naked, the homeless and all those people who feel unwanted, unloved, uncared for throughout society. She built the foundation of 610 missionaries operating in 123 countries being managed by more than 4000 nuns.

Without doubt as any other human being. She have made some incorrect decisions in her life. She end up her life by living for others by doing humanitarian work. Her actions spoke louder than the words of her critics. A master and final salute to the woman who showed the world what a person can do anything if he\ she has a believe in them

A famous quote said by mother Teresa

'Peace begin with a smile' -she lived it,

All these heroes are true leader a lived forever

Don't get success by giving harm, pain to other for own your benefits. Learn good habits

Interview

Learn from others prospective, How top leaders thinks, learn from their experiences

Deepak Ramola

Founder- Project fuel, TED speaker

According to you what is success?

I believe each day brings with itself many battles to be fought, many obstacles to be overcome and many heartbreaks to live through. If you go to bed and wake up to see a new morning, you are successful. That is a proof that you succeeded in putting behind whatever bothered you yesterday and now you have shown up for all that the new day is in store.

How will you define your life (in few words?)

.My life is a constellation of dreams, ideas, experiences, stories, and blessings

What is a quality of a true leader? (According to you)

The quality of a true leader is to lead by example. One must be able to swim in the mud and celebrate small beginnings. You cannot tell others to do as you say and not as you do. You must have experienced what you wish others to undergo. .

Who is your idol?

I am inspired by many people, from all walks of life. But some known influencers in my life have been Oprah Winfrey, Maya Angelou, and Gulzar Sahab.

What are the most common problem in life and what is its solution according to you?

The most common problem in life is holding a grudge for too long. That bitterness can be towards to people who have hurt you, disappointed you or have betrayed you or it can be even towards oneself. The suggestion I can offer is to resolve all your conflicts as soon as you can. The complexities of the things that happen in life cannot outshine the simplicity of life overall. Acknowledging and practicing this philosophy has served me in the toughest of times.

What are the most common problem in life and what is its solution according to you?

The most common problem in life is holding a grudge for too long. That bitterness can be towards to people who have hurt you, disappointed you or have betrayed you or it can be even towards oneself. The suggestion I can offer is to resolve all your conflicts as soon as you can. The complexities of the things that happen in life cannot outshine the simplicity of life overall. Acknowledging and practicing this philosophy has served me in the toughest of times.

What lessons you want to give to your youngster's/ friends.

You always have an extra minute to be nice to somebody. All goodbyes lead you to new hellos, be open. Drink a lot of water.

Laxman Rao

Author, TED speaker

According to you what is success.

Achieving your goals in the future, which you plan in past-defines success

How will you define your life (in few words?)

Life is full of struggles, but do not consider struggle as a problem, stay confident and do not fear of struggle, as they are the part of success.
Considering problem as a problem is the big problem

What are the most important things to make your life - a change?

Experience (Is the most important teacher)

What are the most common problem in life and what is its solution according to you?

A sequence which can be achieved, fulfilled is life. Dream to be big

Who is your idol?

No one is my idol, Book of Gulshan Nanda inspires me to be a successful author

Nikhil Chandwani

Author, TED speaker

According to you what is success?
Success is thank you coming unexpected from people who saw confusion in their life before and through little part in their journey, this brings me the brightest smile and the art of giving is really a beautiful feeling.

How will you define your life?
My life is a training course. Every day I wake up and try to train my emotions. Training emotions helps me channelizing thoughts on a piece of paper and that help me in writing, emotions are indeed the unanswered question in life, surprisingly I was able to balance emotions through the art of giving.

What are the most important things to make your life-a change?
Important component is the people I admire as a part of my journey. Transforming a dull day into a happening one for my parents, my lifeline, and my team is my important ingredient

Who is your idol?
Nature is my idol, I idolize the law of nature that states that the strong survives and weak dies. Emotions strength brings home success and the fear of failure brings death

What are the most common problem in life and what is its solution according to you?
Identity crisis. People are visibly confused and lazy because they don't knows their potential. They can't identify themselves in the crowd and I believe it can be solved through creativity approach in life.

What lessons you want to give to your youngster's/ friends.
Life is a blessing when passion stand tall. No one fails of trying until the last breath for dream that you trust on

Shakshi Holkar

Bollywood singer

According to you, what is Success?

Success! I think every person think differently about being successful in Life and in Defining Success. I personally think that Luxurious lifestyle or Materialistic Achievement is not Being Successful or Achieving Success at all. According to me being Successful is when you're satisfied from yourself. When you achieve the goal you had set up for yourself .Achieving Real Success is all about Being happy with Yourself And Growing as person and making a world Better place for others to live.
"Success is when you reach your destination and you look back and say Journey Was Beautiful."

How will you Define Your Life? (In Few words)

I think my Life is Full of Music, Art and passion. Without Music, My life is incomplete. I have always been the most into music. I had seen many ups and downs in my Life But music always Helped. I think our day defines our Life. So never waste our day. A single day should not be wasted. That's where you shape your life.

What are the most important things to make your life - a change?

According to me for any person it is very necessary to activate some positive changes in our Life. So you need to focus on
•Finding the Meaning of life. Knowing what exactly you want, what is Important and why is it important to you.
•Setting a goal and trying to achieve it in every possible

and positive way. Working hard for them without Cheating.
•To not run after Money and luxuries rather running for a Strong relationships.
•To face your fear. Fighting with your fears and to move forward. It is our fears in life that stop us from living our life to the fullest.
•To Forgive and never regret at your decisions is also a positive change in your life.
•Try to learn and explore. Learning is a process which has no limits. You can learn in many ways and from anyone in any age.

Quality of true leader (Acc. to you)

A good leader can explain his feelings in a positive way. He Himself should be positive and calm. He can keep his point in a perfect way and on right time. A true leader is never afraid of failures. A person who can execute plans in a Proper manner is a true leader according to me.

Who is your idol?

I do not have any particular person to say my idol. My father really has been an inspiration for me since my childhood, I get inspired by lots of people I meet on a daily basis. There are many Handicapped Artists who are blind or Dealing with any other problem inspire me a lot by Their Attitude of "Never Ending Hope". They still work hard and try to prove themselves.

What are the most common problem in life and what is its solution acc. to you?

I Think Time management is a common problem faced by many people. Every second of our Life is very important in achieving success and maintaining Relations. I myself being a musician Sometimes face this problems. Concerts, recordings and shoots Makes my schedule really hectic But

I try that it should not affect my relations and for that we *need to make a schedule and Follow it.*

What message you want to give to our Youngster friends?

I think to all the youngsters who are planning their future and trying to achieve success. I just want to tell them that Work hard Success will follow you. There is no short cut or high jump to achieve success. Hard work is the only way. Channelize your energy and put all of it in your task.

Ankita Sirker

Author

According to you what is success?

Never let anyone else define success for you. Find your own definitions as of me, being successful is being happy in what I do. Success is the first drop of water you taste after long run.

How will you define your life (in few words?)

Have you ever been on a roller coaster ride? My life has been a roller coaster ride, but somehow I have always been able to land on my feet and still do what I love – writes (exactly defines)

What are the most important things to make your life - a change?

You have time to grow and change your life. The season where you figure out what you want from life and thus making a change, consider breaking your goals down in achievable action step. Don't expect yourself to be different overnight, give yourself grace for the process and take small steps daily towards your goals.

What is success?

I define success as living my true purpose, having a positive impact on lives of people by uplifting them and inspiring them incessantly to think and act in way that they may not have considered before

What is a quality of a true leader?

Well, the term "leader" is slightly misleading, a leader is a person who is supposed to walk alongside people, helps them to find the right way, motivate people

Who is your idol?

Well, that's a tricky question. My idol is Khaled Hosseini and JK Rowling.

What are the most common problem in life and what is its solution according to you?

Everybody has problem. Everyone has to face challenges in their lives. That's how things works there exist one solution though: Calm your emotion. Make a decision or solving a problem, take a moment to feel calm. Take a deep breath so that you feel centered and relaxed before moving forward with the problem. So, take a break. Breathe work on things that will actually benefit you as a human being The rest will fall in peace

What lessons you want to give to your youngster's/ friends

Life is what you decide to make it. All the good and bad experiences are responsible to make you the person that you are today. Be great full about it and try to explore more. Go out and make some mistake, fall, and cry. However, once you make the mistake never repeat the same one again. In the end, you will satisfied that you had a life full of experiences and not boredom. Keep yourself motivated, remember just you failed once, doesn't mean you can never succeed –have patience and perseverance. Be optimistic, be a seeker of knowledge and experience, further remember that no one can stop you from achieving your dream.

Dilip Sharma

Blogger

According to you what is a success?

Success is going back to bed, smiling, that you have done something today that was worth doing
Success is undoubtedly different from achievement; don't confuse of achievement as a success. Achievement is the checkpoint we get to and usually term as a success.
Success is a journey, not a destination

How will you define your life (in a few words?)

Everyone thinks that they are different but rather to say like this the better will be to say that everybody is the product of their surroundings.
So my; life addition of my surrounding...

What are the most important things to make your life - a change?

Peace of mind (peace of mind is a new wealth) today's world is about stress, rush, where the peace that everyone desires

What is a success?

When you look back, if you don't have any regret, you are successful

What is the quality of a true leader?

A true leader is a person who can unite the team even in the worst situations. A true leader has integrity, simplicity, passion, courage

Who is your idol?

I don't believe in copying instead I follow some of the great leaders just to get inspired; I have my own ideas to innovate and strategy to apply I am not the number-1 but the only one.

What is the most common problem in life, and what is its solution according to you?

When people are young, they try to set higher unrealistic goal like becoming a space scientist or famous personalities of the world without realizing the current situation but when they grow up goals become smaller like getting decent paying jobs, as probably thinks they are safe, secure , and more beneficial to them and they fail to meet the two ends

They mainly missed persistence in their life. We fail, or the situations sometimes make us forget our capabilities- that what we're capable of, with some minor failure, we tend to forget the goals-which we set in childhood.

But people who keep their eyes on goal follow their daily schedule to reach their goal are successful. Persistence is the key, relies on it

What lessons you want to give to your youngster's/ friends.

I would suggest to read more book and get yourself ahead in every walk of life.

"Books are the source of life's lessons."

Hari Shankar Tripathi

Experienced Teacher, excellent personality

According to you what is a success?

Achieving, desire with determination, honesty, practice, and hard work goal determines the success.

How will you define your life?

There was a lot of struggle in my early days, with the help of my parents I completed my post graduations from Allahabad, and today I am fulfilled and happy with my life.

I have seen a lot of struggle in early life to till date and learn great lessons.

What is the quality of a true leader?

A leader is one who thinks about everyone, the one who thinks about all the citizens of the society-from poor to rich class. And moreover should be honest.

Who is your idol?

My idol was Atal Bihari Vajpayee as a prime minister and as a leader.

What is the most common problem in life, and what is its solution according to you?

There are unlimited, never-ending wishes of people exist and is as vast as the sea. Once in my early day, I read a poem as

Life of human are as vast as the sea, a man wants to cross the sea of desire through a frail boat...

Alas!! A man reaches the end of his life, but the wish remains unfilled

What lessons you want to give to your youngster's/ friends.

Achieve success through honesty, inherit the character of caring

For the winner in YOU

Write your own thoughts

According to you what is a success?

How will you define your life (in a few words?)

What are the most important things to make your life - a change?

What is the quality of a true leader?

Who is your idol?

What lessons you want to give to your youngster's/ friends.

FAILURE

Let Us defeat it

Aim - To defeat the defeat before it defeat you

Objective – To attain high success from failure

To learn from failure

To become a true leader

A general view or **about-** 1. A general idea and awareness

2. Strategy

3. Conclusion

Nobody wants to fails, but it is necessary to fail, if you want to succeed same as it is necessary to be defocus before to get focused

Failure defeat losers, inspire winners

While some people have fear of failure-

Note:-

-Failure is the part of success

-Failure is not final

Every successful person in row, have a great failure stories.

Read those story to get inspire from it.

The main difference between inspiration and motivation is that - *motivation is short term, and inspiration is long term*

Secondly motivation depends on outdoor factor whereas inspiration comes from your inner world

Never copy other every person, as he or she have own ***capability****, and importantly the situation will never be the same as you compare, so just inspire from successful person*

One should not dwell upon his failures rather quickly tries to find out the ways to achieve.

You didn't get fail, your plan actually get fails, your plan was not appropriates

Prepare your plan according to your ability

-You may heard this statement several times

But actually,

NOT!!

Prepare your plan out of your ability – so that step by step, day by day, you will reach and be a high scorer in every way and exponentially increase your graph rapidly, And one day your will be limitless.

A man fails 100 times but doesn't quit at all, tries and tries, has a passion to work exceptionally, he founded the great electric bulb.

Thomas Alva Edison

He used to work in petrol bunks, became one of the wealthiest person of India

Dhirubhai Ambani

Mr. Avul Pakir Jainulabdeen Abdul Kalam has a dearest dream to become fighter pilot but get rejected over the year, Mr. Abdul Kalam writes- I had nurtured the hope to be able to fly to handle a machine as it rose higher and higher in the stratosphere was my dearest dream.
But I fails to relies, my dream

Later known as a missile man of India for his contribution in ballistic missile, and to India's Pokhran-II nuclear test in 1998 make him great or mahatma Abdul Kalam,, more over a prominent Indian scientist who served as a 11th president of India,

Mr. Abdul Kalam

People used to say-

Only w0men can cook food

Sanjev Kapoor

Story starts from zero and end as a hero

Official age of retirement is 58, but he started after 58, rejected for a job in All India radio because of this height, baritone and heavy voice

But now the voice of million aspirations, iconic status and proves as a real example of perseverance

Amitabh Bachchan

Came from a very normal family saw a lot of failure in life. At early age my parents died, I equated poverty with failure

He wanted to be a sports man but didn't stuck up to it and moved on. His success and failure both story motivates us.

People used to say

Only actor's son can become a successful actor

Shahrukh khan

If you aren't scared enough of failing you are unlikely to succeed

---

Used to sleep on the floor in friends room, getting weekly meal by traveling many kilometers to the way of temple.

Steve jobs

His teacher calls him slow he also didn't speak until he turned 4 and didn't read until he was 7 years.

Albert Einstein

Who has a dream of writing novel-?

Once completed, twelve publishing house initially rejected the manuscript. Fortunately a small publishing house agreed to publish the book finally,

JK Rowling became an international best Selling author and best Selling book in the history.-First female to become a billionaire author.

Wrote the most famous book "Harry Potter" that proves - : magic beyond words.

JK Rowling.

Failure meant a stripping away of the in essential. I stopped pretending to myself that I was anything other than what I was, I began to direct all my energy to finishing the only work that matter to me. Had I really succeed at anything else, I might never have found the determination to succeed in the one area where I truly belonged. I was set free, because my greatest fear had been realized, and I was still alive, and I still had a daughter whom I adore, and I had an old typewriter, and a big idea. And so rock bottom become a solid foundation on which I rebuild my life

\- **JK Rowling**

His act was initially rejected by Hollywood studios because they felt it was too nonsensical to ever sell

But now consider as one of the greatest filmmaker in the history in the history of American cinema, whose movies were and still are popular throughout the world.

Charlie Chaplin

Write a reason on a page *asking yourself* -why you fails in …….

-stick that page on a wall near you, before you, around you, where you can look at that every time everyday regularly, learn a biggest lesson from it …

Failure is not final

Now talking about the people,

The people who fails and has a fear of failure probably thinks like this -

What the people will think about me?

What will I do?

How I can prove myself?

I think I am a failure

I can't do anything

Really I don't have a brain

Why people called me as a failure?

But you should rather think like this

How can I be successful?

How will I make my play to achieve great height?

Next time.

Be fast, be smart and an achiever to excel

Here is the way that can change you from failure to achiever.

(Every sentence has a great meaning and deep thinking required)

1. **Believe you can** it is one of the most important thing it is well written that *"if you believe you can, you will but if you believe you can't, you will not"*
2. Have a great plan and a strategy
3. Think - it's my last chance to win further I have to prove the world that a genius lies within me
4. Most importantly, you need to be aware and understand the importance of the work you are doing NOW

Answers the followings '*honestly*'-

Clear aim- *write your golden aim*

……………………………..

……………………………………………..

How this work can help me – *the work that you are doing currently, can help you in long run*

……………………………………………………

……………………………………………………

……………………………………………………

Whom you dedicated this –

……………………………………………………

……………………………………………………

5. Read 3rd again
6. Never fear about failure, gain confidence
7. Don't be confuse- ask elder or better to ask person who is itself master in that field
8. Don't argue with other or judge persons quickly tries to take good advice
9. Don't share you plan or work with every one let them hear the voice of your victory
10. Practice, perfect, work smart
11. Don't distract, by the people, everyone has own idea, view, prospective- to look at the world … they will tell different ideas varying from

person to person, you have to make right decision

There is a place reserved, waiting for you to welcome you, only have be capability to achieve or fit at that place.

What the situation will be

The situation may get worst?

You have to travel that path, just follow the above rule, act upon your weakness, and strengthen your strong points -to be unique

Don't worry about society, just believe in yourself- 'Empty vessel, sounds more'!!

At every worst situation, you have a golden opportunity to prove, go and find it quickly

Start from now and whatever you have where you have *don't matter*

Frameworks

Focus-

- Visualize them.
- Work on them.
- Look at them every day.

The right way – Review all of these in case of selecting a goal choose any one, set a deadline to make a great, practically possible plan for it, exercise on it at every day this can create a great impact on your life.

Go to a place in the lap of nature, under full silence where you feel better sit quietly and ask following question to yourself further start by recording from where you are today-

Name-..

Current age -...............

What milestone you see in the future

(How you see yourself after 10 years)-

....

Write your 5 dream-

…………………………………………………………………..

……………………………………………………………………

……………………………………………………………………

…………………………………………………………………..

……………………………………………………………………

……………………………………………………………………

Write the name of your dream place and a travel companion.

……………………………………………………

……………………………………………………

…………………………………………………..

……………………………………………………

NEGATIVE	POSITIVE
~~I can't be a winner~~	……………….
~~I am not smart enough~~	………………..
~~What if I get embarrass~~	……………….
~~Why? I don't have the resources~~	……………….
	………………...
~~Why? People thing negative about me~~	……………
	……………......

.

Jot down your thoughts

……………………………………………………………
……………………………………………………………
……………………………………………………………
……………………………………………………………
……………………………………………………………
……………………………………………………………

Set a deadline for your dream- Date………………..

Year………………

Precautions

You may start to doubt yourself at times. But talk yourself out of this self-defeating behavior. Henry Ford once said, "Whether you think you can or can't, you're right." The power of your thoughts can help or hinder you on your path to success, so reverse any negative speech or thoughts, whether they come from you or someone else. Keep telling yourself you can do it and take focused action to make your dreams a reality.

CONCLUSION

LET ME KNOW YOUR THOUGHTS, REVIEW, AND FEEDBACK

authorankitkumarverma@gmail.com

Ankit_kumar_verma_quotes/Instagram

My thoughts and words are always with you.

THE JOURNEY ENDS HERE YOU MAY GET EXTREME SUCCESS, IMMENSE PLEASURE HAPPINESS AND BEST OF BEST FOR REST OF THE LIFE ...

HAPPY READING